PING PO
KING KONG

Poems by Brian Moses

Illustrated by Lee Wildish

First Flight

Titles in First Flight

Phantom Striker
Pest Control
Shark's Fin Island
Scary!
Ping Pong with King Kong
The Fame Game
Awesome Animals
Big, Fast Rides
Car Boot Genie
Monster Cards
Ssh! My Family are Spies
Ghost Dog Mystery
Chip Boy
Sky Bikers
Surfing Three-Sixty
Something in the Kitchen
The Ghost in the Art Room
Robert and the Werewolf
The Biggest Lies Ever
Mad about Money

Badger Publishing Limited
Oldmedow Road, Hardwick Industrial Estate,
King's Lynn PE30 4JJ
Telephone: 01438 791037
www.badgerlearning.co.uk

2 4 6 8 10 9 7 5 3

Ping Pong with King Kong ISBN 978 1 84424 821 6

First edition © 2006
This second edition © 2013

Series Editor: Jonny Zucker
Publisher: David Jamieson
Commissioning Editor: Carrie Lewis
Editor: Paul Martin
Design: Fiona Grant
Illustration: Lee Wildish

PING PONG WITH KING KONG

Poems by Brian Moses

Contents

Badger
LEARNING

Playing Ping Pong with King Kong

To play ping pong with King Kong,
you must be in good shape.
Be sure to run each day
and you may just beat this ape.

Just keep your eye on the game,
and don't look at his face.
King Kong will try to hit the ball
all around the place.

King Kong is good at ping pong,
and he knows just what to do.
Very soon this ape may make
a monkey out of you!

Bouncing Babies

Why do we say that babies bounce
when they don't?
We could say, what a lovely,
bouncing frog, or grasshopper,
or kangaroo.
But we don't.

We say, “What a lovely bouncing baby,” and babies don’t.
You can’t bounce a baby along the ground and then lob her into a net!

You can't hold on, and
bounce her along like a
spacehopper!

Babies don't bounce.
So don't ever try,
I'm not telling a lie, they don't...

Keeping Fit

Sunday – fun run day.
Monday – slim tum day.
Tuesday – lose flab day.
Wednesday – knees bend day.
Thursday – work out day.
Friday – skip high day
Saturday – so tired day!

zzzzzz.....

The Overtaker

I'm an overtaker,
off down the line.
I don't wait around,
I haven't got time.

I'm an overtaker,
I can't stay back.
I'm out in front,
ahead of the pack.

Better keep clear
in the swimming bath.
Everybody
out of my path.

I'm an overtaker,
watch me run.
Every sports day,
sound of the gun.

There I go,
off down the track.
Nothing is going
to hold me back.

Head in the clouds,
I don't look round.
Keep my feet
clear of the ground.

Run to school,
every day.
Any old race,
I'm okay.

Dash home at night,
have lots of fun.
I'm an overtaker,
watch me rrrrr.................un!

Out-Time, In-Time

Out-time, out-time,
run around and shout time,
shake it all about time,
out-time, out-time.

In-time, in-time,
did you lose or win time?
Chuck it in the bin time,
in-time, in-time.

Out-time, out-time,
have a knock about time,
give your friend a clout time,
out-time, out-time.

In-time, in-time,
it's time to begin time,
stop the noisy din time,
in-time, in-time.

10

The Body Shop

Why did the skeleton cross
the road?

To get to the Body Shop!

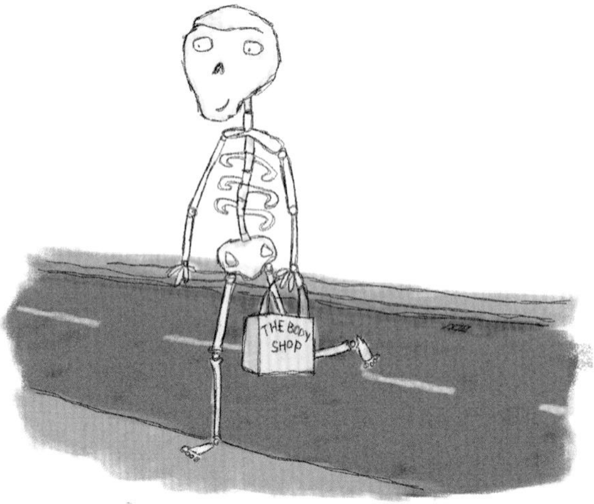

When you run out of steam
and are about to stop,
just get yourself down
to the Body Shop.

When you're out of puff
and you start to flop,
just get yourself down
to the Body Shop.

They’ve got
lots of new feet,
knees that won’t crack,
hands that move fast
and a bendier back.

Heads full of hair,
tums that are slim.
Long long legs
to help you swim.

A tiny nose?
No trouble at all.
Non sticky-out ears?
Just give them a call.

Oh the Body Shop!
That's the place to stop.
Just get yourself down
to the Body Shop.

Just get yourself down
to the Body Shop.

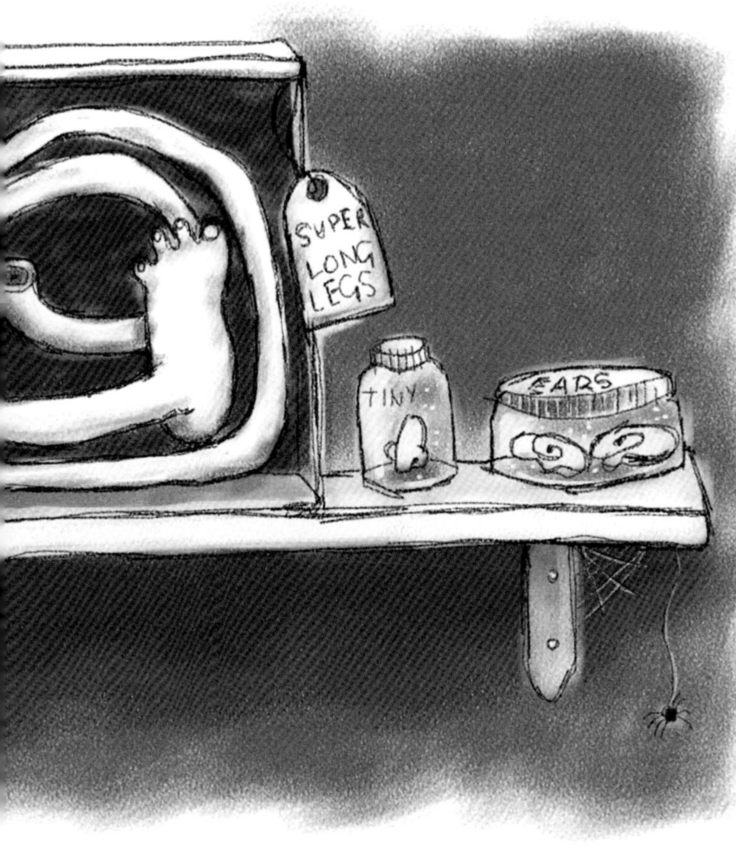

Superhero

I'd like to be a superhero,
I'd like to fly through the sky.
I'd like to sit on the roof
and watch the birds fly by.

I'd like to be James Bond
and drive a big fast car.
I'd like to play for Man U.
and be a football star.

Or maybe sing songs on TV,
that would be really cool.
So each day I sit and dream
and pretend I'm not at school.

MAN U

Leg It!

Leg it, leg it, leg it,
leg it as fast as you can.

Leg it to the end of the street,
leg it, pick up your feet.

Leg it, can't you hear them shout.
Leg it, go on, get out!

Leg it, I can't wait for you,
leg it, I'm coming through.

Leg it, I don't want to be
kissed by Samantha Dee!

Sky Football

Outside a pub
a sign said:
Sky Football.

But how do you play
a game like that?

Do you fly
down the pitch?

Do you boot the ball
into clouds?

Do you dribble it
between stars?

JETS
5

Do you hear the cheers of angels
as you score a goal?

Just how do you play
Sky Football?

I'm no good at football,
I'm no good at cricket.
I'm no good at running.
I'm no good at swimming.
I'm no good at snooker.
I'm no good at darts.

But if there were sports
like spending money,
eating at parties
or fighting my sister,

If there were sports
like nose picking
or nail biting,
face pulling
or pinching....

I'd be the winner!

Boxing Kangaroo

If a boxing kangaroo
one day, runs away from the zoo.
Don't try to stop it,
or get in its way,
for it might pick a fight with you.

And a boxing kangaroo,
will be better at fighting than you.
If he gives you a smack,
your eye will be black,
and you'll feel very silly too!